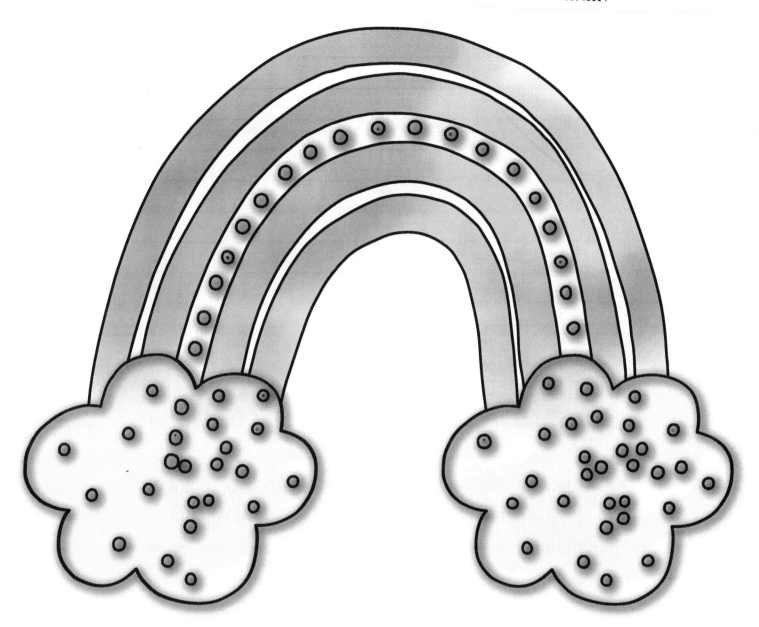

FREAKY RAINBOWS

A Coloring Book for Kids and Adult

Test your rainbow colours

Are you ready? Here we go...!

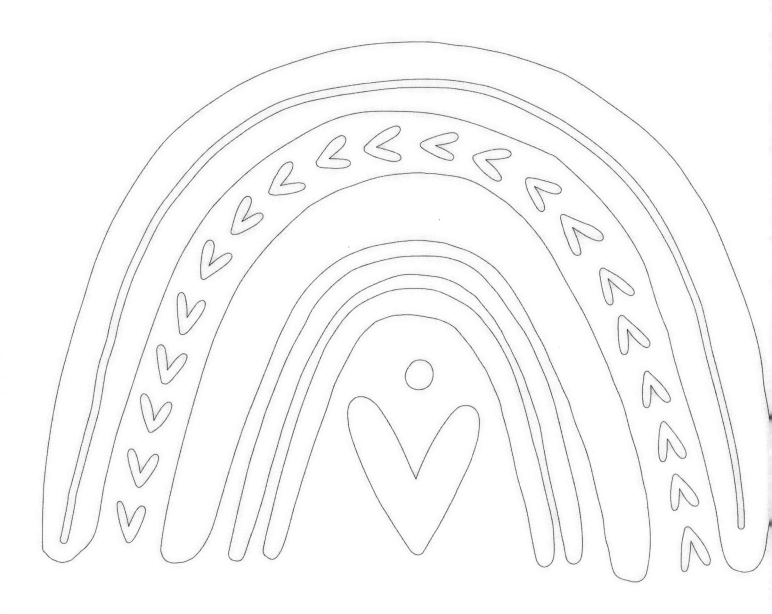

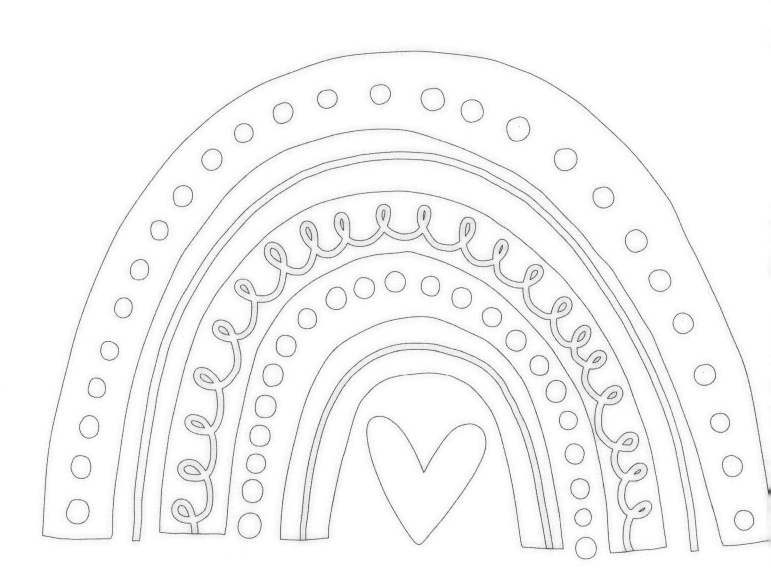

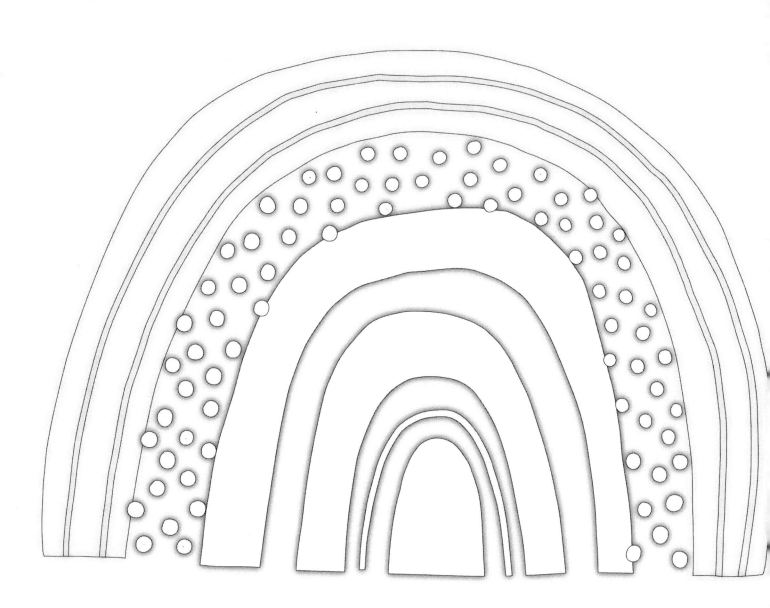

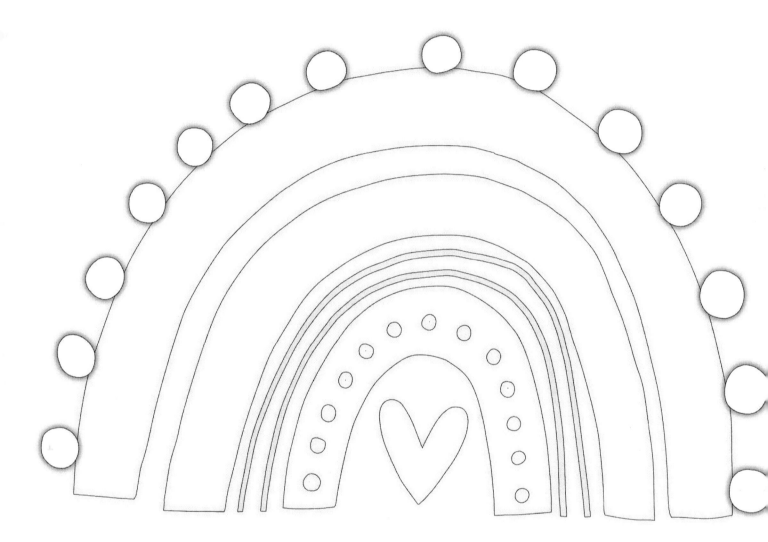

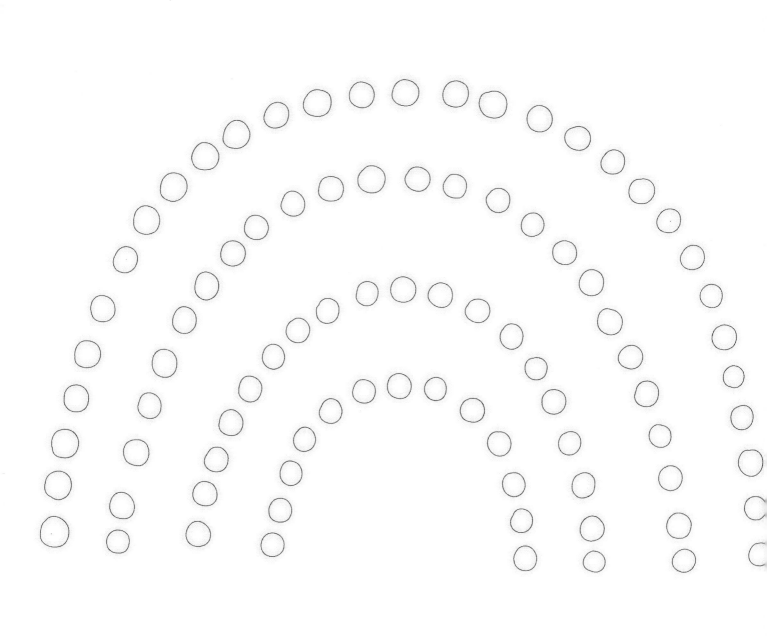

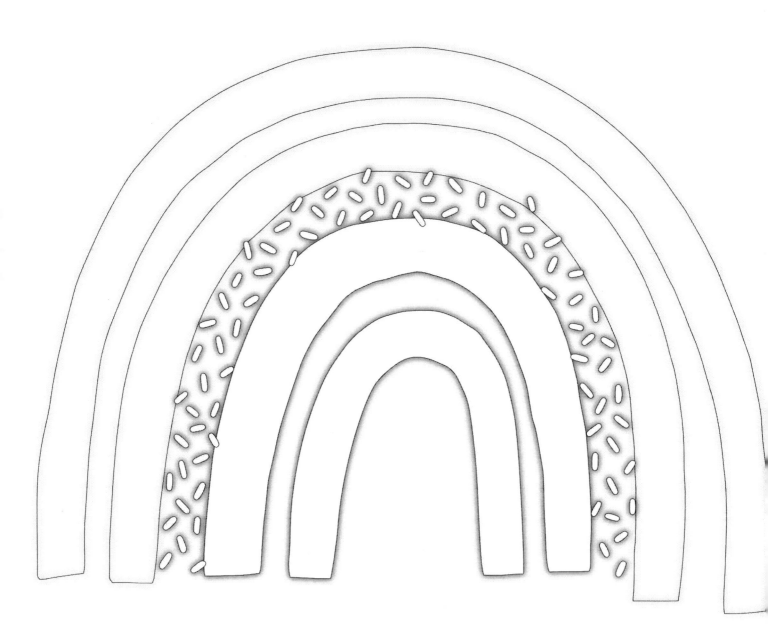

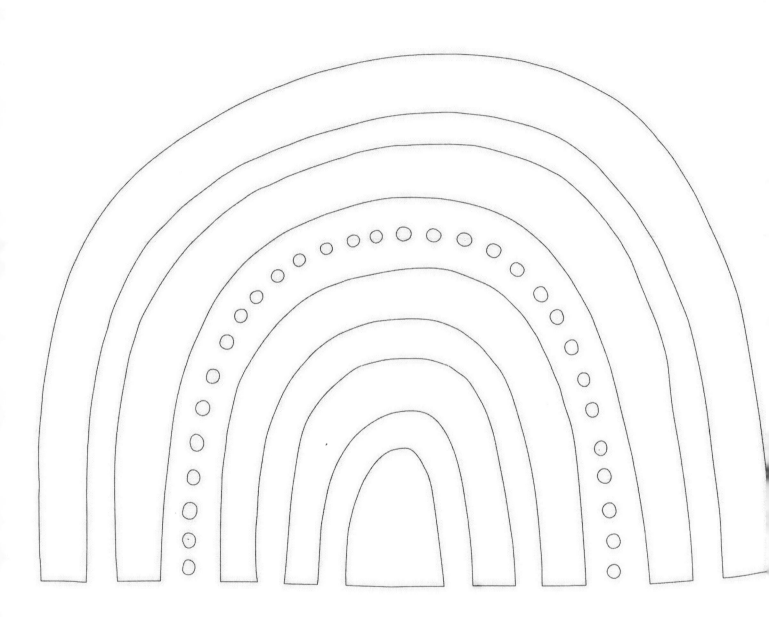

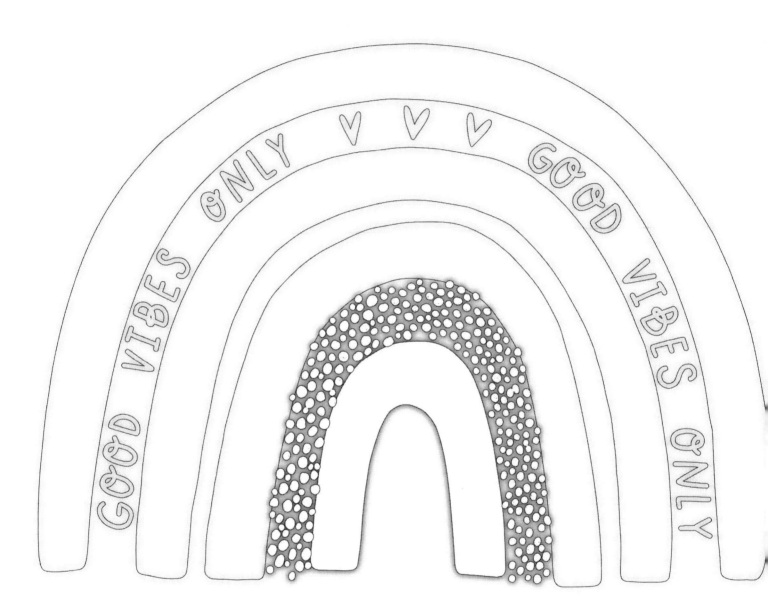

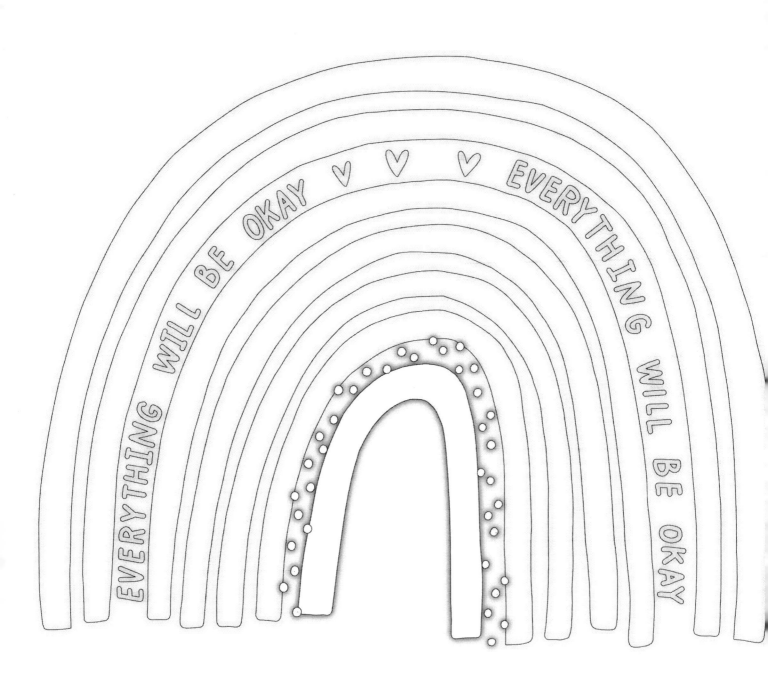

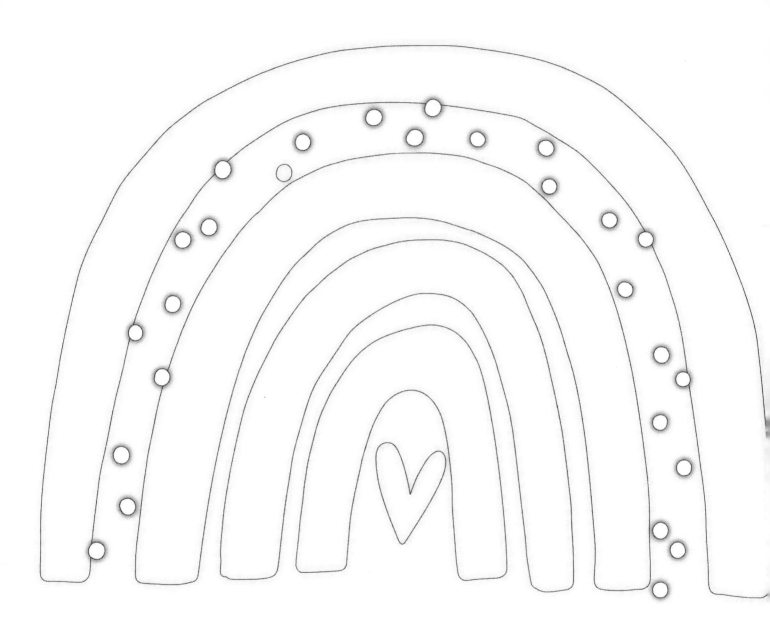

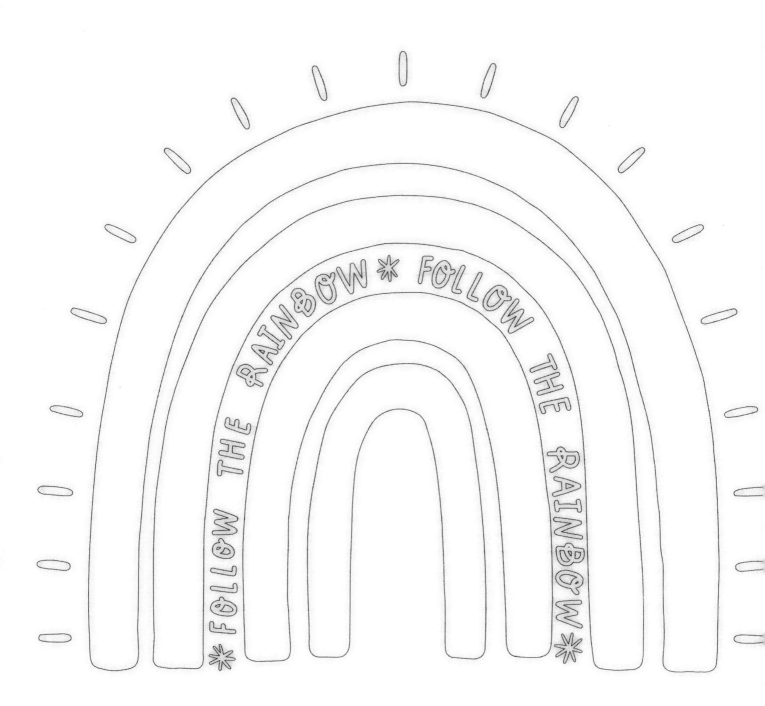

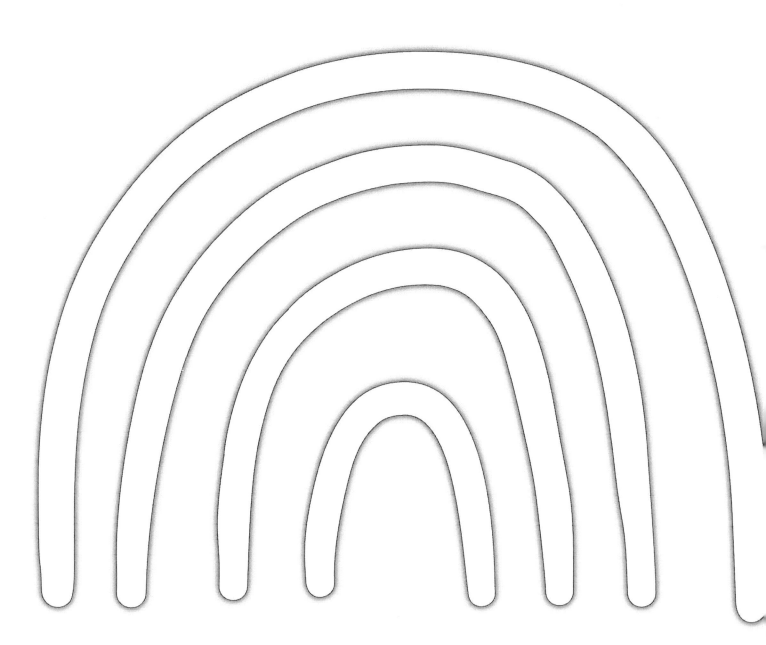

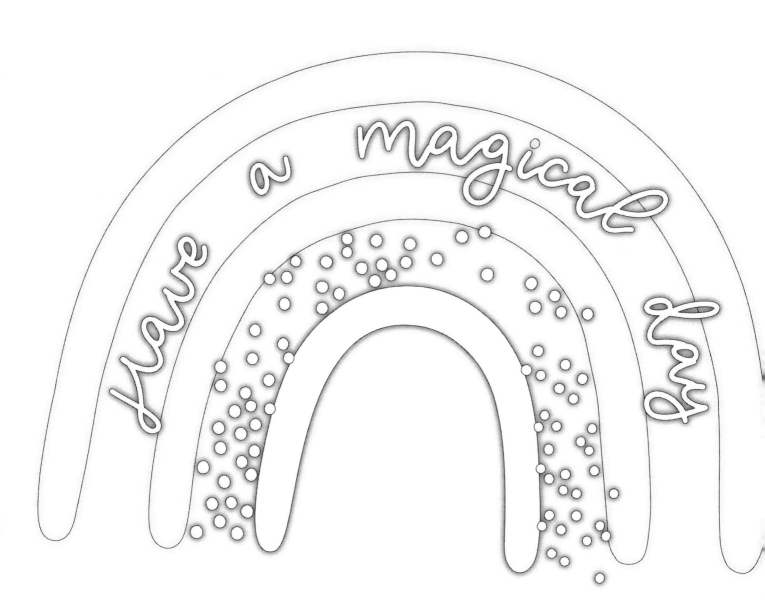

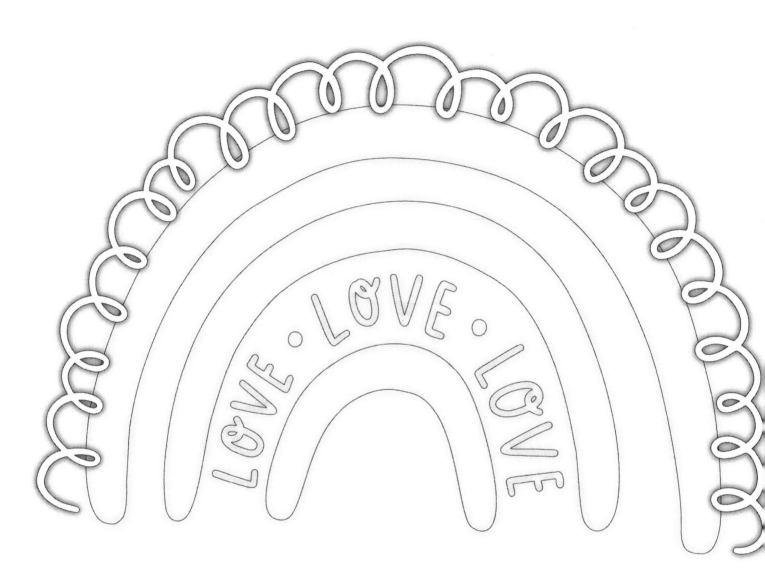

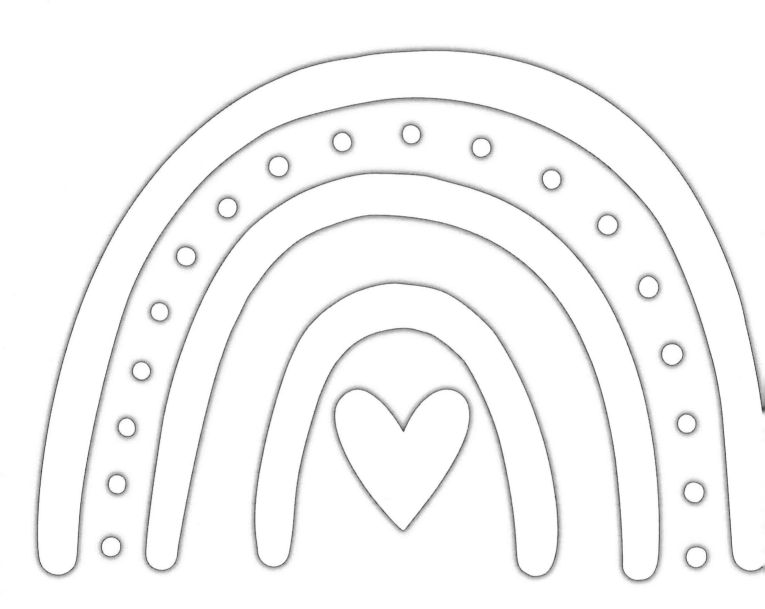

HAVE YOU PAINTED IN ALL THE RAINBOWS?
I HOPE YOU HAD A LOT OF FUN DOING THAT!

Made in the USA
Columbia, SC
28 May 2020